Francis Frith's

East London

Photographic Memories

Francis Frith's
East London

Leigh Hatts

First published in the United Kingdom in 2000 by
Frith Book Company Ltd

Hardback Edition 2000
ISBN 1-85937-080-2

Paperback Edition 2001
ISBN 1-85937-475-1

Reprinted in Hardback 2001
ISBN 1-85937-080-2

British Library Cataloguing in Publication Data

Francis Frith's East London
Leigh Hatts

Frith Book Company Ltd
Frith's Barn, Teffont,
Salisbury, Wiltshire SP3 5QP
Tel: +44 (0) 1722 716 376
Email: info@francisfrith.co.uk
www.francisfrith.co.uk

Printed and bound in Great Britain

AS WITH ANY HISTORICAL DATABASE THE FRITH ARCHIVE IS CONSTANTLY BEING CORRECTED AND IMPROVED
AND THE PUBLISHERS WOULD WELCOME INFORMATION ON OMISSIONS OR INACCURACIES

Contents

Francis Frith: *Victorian Pioneer*

FRANCIS FRITH, Victorian founder of the world-famous photographic archive, was a complex and multi-talented man. A devout Quaker and a highly successful Victorian businessman, he was both philosophic by nature and pioneering in outlook.

By 1855 Francis Frith had already established a wholesale grocery business in Liverpool, and sold it for the astonishing sum of £200,000, which is the equivalent today of over £15,000,000. Now a multi-millionaire, he was able to indulge his passion for travel. As a child he had pored over travel books written by early explorers, and his fancy and imagination had been stirred by family holidays to the sublime mountain regions of Wales and Scotland. 'What a land of spirit-stirring and enriching scenes and places!' he had written. He was to return to these scenes of grandeur in later years to 'recapture the thousands of vivid and tender memories', but with a different purpose. Now in his thirties, and captivated by the new science of photography, Frith set out on a series of pioneering journeys to the Nile regions that occupied him from 1856 until 1860.

Intrigue and Adventure

He took with him on his travels a specially-designed wicker carriage that acted as both dark-room and sleeping chamber. These far-flung journeys were packed with intrigue and adventure. In his life story, written when he was sixty-three, Frith tells of being held captive by bandits, and of fighting 'an awful midnight battle to the very point of surrender with a deadly pack of hungry, wild dogs'. Sporting flowing Arab costume, Frith arrived at Akaba by camel seventy years before Lawrence, where he encountered 'desert princes and rival sheikhs, blazing with jewel-hilted swords'.

During these extraordinary adventures he was assiduously exploring the desert regions bordering the Nile and patiently recording the antiquities and peoples with his camera. He was the first photographer to venture beyond the sixth cataract. Africa was still the mysterious 'Dark Continent', and Stanley and Livingstone's historic meeting was a decade into the future. The conditions for picture taking confound belief. He laboured for hours in his wicker dark-room in the sweltering heat of the desert, while the volatile chemicals fizzed dangerously in their trays. Often he was forced to work in remote tombs and caves where conditions were cooler. Back in London he exhibited his photographs and was 'rapturously cheered' by members of the Royal Society. His reputation as a photographer was made overnight. An eminent modern historian has likened their impact on the population of the time to that on our own generation of the first photographs taken on the surface of the moon.

Venture of a Life-Time

Characteristically, Frith quickly spotted the opportunity to create a new business as a specialist publisher of photographs. He lived in an era of immense and sometimes violent change. For the poor in the early part of Victoria's reign work was a drudge and the hours long, and people had precious little free time to enjoy themselves. Most had no transport other than a cart or gig at their disposal, and had not travelled far beyond the boundaries of their own town or village. However, by the 1870s, the railways had threaded their way across the country, and Bank Holidays and half-day Saturdays had been made obligatory by Act of Parliament. All of a sudden the ordinary working man and his family were able to enjoy days out and see a little more of the world.

With characteristic business acumen, Francis Frith foresaw that these new tourists would enjoy having souvenirs to commemorate their days out. In 1860 he married Mary Ann Rosling and set out with the intention of photographing every city, town and village in Britain. For the next thirty years he travelled the country by train and by pony and trap, producing fine photographs of seaside resorts and beauty spots that were keenly bought by millions of Victorians. These prints were painstakingly pasted into family albums and pored over during the dark nights of winter, rekindling precious memories of summer excursions.

The Rise of Frith & Co

Frith's studio was soon supplying retail shops all over the country. To meet the demand he gathered about him a small team of photographers, and published the work of independent artist-photographers of the calibre of Roger Fenton and Francis Bedford. In order to gain some understanding of the scale of Frith's business one only has to look at the catalogue issued by Frith & Co in 1886: it runs to some 670 pages, listing not only many thousands of views of the British Isles but also many photographs of most European countries, and China, Japan, the USA and

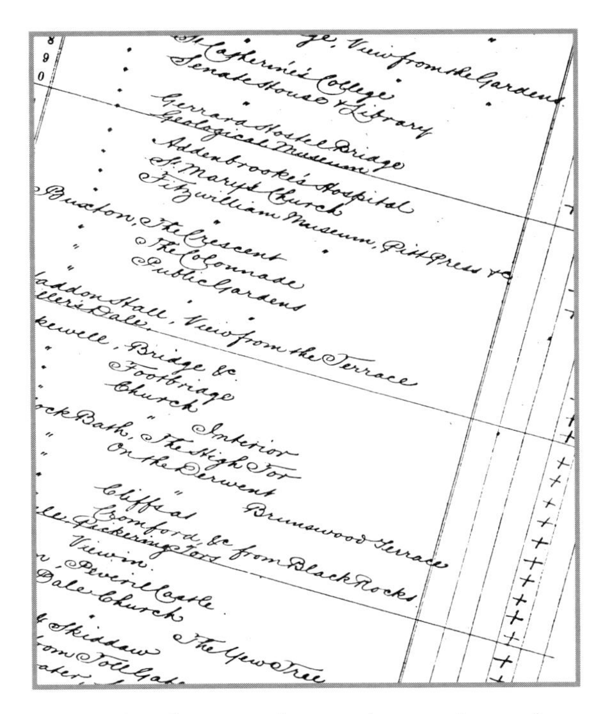

ge, View from the Garden
St Catherine's College
Senate House & Library
Gerrard Hostel Bridge
Geological Museum
Addenbrooke's Hospital
St. Mary's Church
Fitzwilliam Museum, Pitt Press &c
Buxton, The Crescent
The Colonnade
Public Gardens
Haddon Hall, View from the Terrace
llers Dale
kewell, Bridge &c.
Footbridge
Church
ck Bath, The High Tor
" Interior
On the Derwent
Cliffs at
" Brunswood Terrace
Cromford, &c from Black Rocks
le Pickering Tors
View in
n, Peveril Castle
Dale Church
Skiddaw
The Yew Tree
rom Toll Gate

Canada – note the sample page shown above from the hand-written *Frith & Co* ledgers detailing pictures taken. By 1890 Frith had created the greatest specialist photographic publishing company in the world, with over 2,000 outlets – more than the combined number that Boots and WH Smith have today! The picture on the right shows the *Frith & Co* display board at Ingleton in the Yorkshire Dales. Beautifully constructed with mahogany frame and gilt inserts, it could display up to a dozen local scenes.

Postcard Bonanza

The ever-popular holiday postcard we know today took many years to develop. In 1870 the Post Office issued the first plain cards, with a pre-printed stamp on one face. In 1894 they allowed other publishers' cards to be sent through the mail with an attached adhesive halfpenny stamp. Demand grew rapidly, and in 1895 a new size of postcard was permitted called the court card, but there was little room for illustration. In 1899, a year after Frith's death, a new card measuring 5.5 x 3.5 inches became the standard format, but it was not until 1902 that the divided back came into being, with address and message on one face and a full-size illustration on the other. *Frith & Co* were in the vanguard of postcard development, and Frith's sons Eustace and Cyril continued their father's monumental task, expanding the number of views offered to the public and recording more and more places in Britain, as the coasts and countryside were opened up to mass travel.

Francis Frith died in 1898 at his villa in Cannes, his great project still growing. The archive he created continued in business for another seventy years. By 1970 it contained over a third of a million pictures of 7,000 cities, towns and villages. The massive photographic record Frith has left to us stands as a living monument to a special and very remarkable man.

Frith's Archive: *A Unique Legacy*

FRANCIS FRITH'S legacy to us today is of immense significance and value, for the magnificent archive of evocative photographs he created provides a unique record of change in 7,000 cities, towns and villages throughout Britain over a century and more. Frith and his fellow studio photographers revisited locations many times down the years to update their views, compiling for us an enthralling and colourful pageant of British life and character.

We tend to think of Frith's sepia views of Britain as nostalgic, for most of us use them to conjure up memories of places in our own lives with which we have family associations. It often makes us forget that to Francis Frith they were records of daily life as it was actually being lived in the cities, towns and villages of his day. The Victorian age was one of great and often bewildering change for ordinary people, and though the pictures evoke an impression of slower times, life was as busy and hectic as it is today.

See Frith at www.francisfrith.co.uk

We are fortunate that Frith was a photographer of the people, dedicated to recording the minutiae of everyday life. For it is this sheer wealth of visual data, the painstaking chronicle of changes in dress, transport, street layouts, buildings, housing, engineering and landscape that captivates us so much today. His remarkable images offer us a powerful link with the past and with the lives of our ancestors.

Today's Technology

Computers have now made it possible for Frith's many thousands of images to be accessed almost instantly. In the Frith archive today, each photograph is carefully 'digitised' then stored on a CD Rom. Frith archivists can locate a single photograph amongst thousands within seconds. Views can be catalogued and sorted under a variety of categories of place and content to the immediate benefit of researchers.

Inexpensive reference prints can be created for them at the touch of a mouse button, and a wide range of books and other printed materials assembled and published for a wider, more general readership - in the next twelve months over a hundred Frith local history titles will be published! The day-to-day workings of the archive are very different from how they were in Francis Frith's time: imagine the herculean task of sorting through eleven tons of glass negatives as Frith had to do to locate a particular sequence of pictures! Yet the archive still prides itself on maintaining the same high standards of excellence laid down by Francis Frith, including the painstaking cataloguing and indexing of every view.

It is curious to reflect on how the internet now allows researchers in America and elsewhere greater instant access to the archive than Frith himself ever enjoyed. Many thousands of individual views can be called up on screen within seconds on one of the Frith internet sites, enabling people living continents away to revisit the streets of their ancestral home town, or view places in Britain where they have enjoyed holidays. Many overseas researchers welcome the chance to view special theme selections, such as transport, sports, costume and ancient monuments.

We are certain that Francis Frith would have heartily approved of these modern developments in imaging techniques, for he himself was always working at the very limits of Victorian photographic technology.

The Value of the Archive Today

Because of the benefits brought by the computer, Frith's images are increasingly studied by social historians, by researchers into genealogy and ancestory, by architects, town planners, and by teachers and schoolchildren involved in local history projects.

In addition, the archive offers every one of us an opportunity to examine the places where we and our families have lived and worked down the years. Highly successful in Frith's own era, the archive is now, a century and more on, entering a new phase of popularity.

The Past in Tune with the Future

Historians consider the Francis Frith Collection to be of prime national importance. It is the only archive of its kind remaining in private ownership and has been valued at a million pounds. However, this figure is now rapidly increasing as digital technology enables more and more people around the world to enjoy its benefits.

Francis Frith's archive is now housed in an historic timber barn in the beautiful village of Teffont in Wiltshire. Its founder would not recognize the archive office as it is today. In place of the many thousands of dusty boxes containing glass plate negatives and an all-pervading odour of photographic chemicals, there are now ranks of computer screens. He would be amazed to watch his images travelling round the world at unimaginable speeds through network and internet lines.

The archive's future is both bright and exciting. Francis Frith, with his unshakeable belief in making photographs available to the greatest number of people, would undoubtedly approve of what is being done today with his lifetime's work. His photographs, depicting our shared past, are now bringing pleasure and enlightenment to millions around the world a century and more after his death.

East London - *An Introduction*

EAST LONDON BEGINS at Aldgate Pump on the boundary of the City of London. The first major building over the border is the Tower of London, which is definitely not in the City of London. The boundary on Tower Hill is beaten every year on Ascension Day by the parish of All Hallows-by-the-Tower within the City, and every third year the Liberty of the Tower is ceremoniously beaten by the Beefeaters and their families. During the ceremony both parties meet to publicly define the line. Indeed, the first modern borough east of the Square Mile is called Tower Hamlets; it embraces Whitechapel Road, which was home to the first large general market beyond the City.

Once, East London could be said to end at Bow Bridge; today, the capital's eastern ecclesiastical boundary is the River Lea. East of the Lea, the Church of England parishes fall within the Diocese of Chelmsford rather than London. Bow Church has its own Bow Bells. Those born in the East End were said to be born within the sound of Bow Bells - either the bells of St Mary-le-Bow in the City of London's Cheapside to the west, or the bells of Bow Church in the far east. Before the arrival of the motor car, church bells could be heard far away.

East London expanded dramatically to embrace rural Essex in 1965 when the Greater London Council was created to administer a wider area than the London County Council. The boroughs have also been amalgamated; for example, Romford's local authority is called Havering, taking its name from Havering-atte-Bower, where kings lived from before the Norman Conquest until the 17th century.

This book, therefore, can look back on a diverse territory, where the pictures prove that London really is a series of villages and hamlets which have linked up. The further east you go, the more you

can find fine survivals of rural life. Indeed, at the furthest Underground station, Upminster, the visitor will even find a windmill.

The pictures of Barking indicate great changes even in recent years. Barking was the seat of William the Conqueror's government after he had been crowned in Westminster Abbey in 1066. The Abbey, on Barking Creek, was in a strategic position; when it was closed by Henry VIII, it had become the most important convent in the country. Even today Barking has a suffragan bishop. The late 20th-century town centre changes have made Barking a shopping centre in its own right, with both a shopping mall and a market.

Further east is the Becontree estate: this was built by the London County Council during the 1920s and early 1930s, and finally completed in 1934. The plan was to encourage Londoners to move east for better housing conditions - with 25,000 homes, it was Europe's largest housing estate. Later building programmes extended the estate to nearly 27,000 homes, with an estimated population of 90,000. The Becontree estate was handy for the expanding Ford Motor works, which opened in 1931. This had a profound affect on Dagenham village. Its ancient church is built on raised ground which still makes a most attractive setting with a pub across the narrow road dating from Tudor times.

Frith has a very valuable archive of photographs for Hornchurch; it began as a priory, which then spawned a village. The pictures clearly capture the last of the buildings which were known to pilgrims travelling south to St Thomas Becket's shrine at Canterbury, and they also capture the rapid transformation of the main street and hinterland with the arrival of the railway and cars.

The new St Leonard's Hamlet takes its name from the parish of St Leonard's, Shoreditch, which built its cottage homes for East End children on the Essex farmland. Only by looking at the old photographs can the name and the layout of today's now redeveloped estate make sense to the resident or visitor.

There is a picture of the Hornchurch windmill, which once looked across the Ingrebourne valley to Upminster's mill. Again, the photographs show the shift of population. Birds Lane has lost its importance, and even its post-box, as the brick and tile industry has given way to the Southend arterial road. The new early 20th-century streets near the station contain the model commuter accommodation which brought Londoners into what was then rural Essex. It is fascinating to see how the gardens have matured, and in most cases improved, despite the temptation to create off-street parking bays. But today there is still enough countryside left for much of the adjacent green land to be designated as a community forest called Thames Chase.

North of Hornchurch is Ardleigh Green, which abuts Gidea Park. These are areas which have long

been ignored, even by London historians. Gidea Park is a suburb of Romford; but its inhabitants are proud of it, for this is a lost garden suburb which attracted the attentions of architects such as Parker & Unwin and Curtis Green. Romford has one of London's oldest and largest market squares, which according to the photographs remains the little-changed focal point; but the immediate surrounding streets have had such dramatic development that even the war memorial has been moved. Above all, the landmark brewery which once gave employment to the small market town has disappeared.

Further down the railway line towards central London is Ilford. Here, not only is the High Road now free of cars, but also a street has even given way to a shopping centre. Ilford is by the Roding Valley, which brings the River Roding down from Epping Forest. This is 'London's back garden', owned by the Corporation of London; it had the foresight to save the forest from developers to be a green lung. One photograph shows Chingford Station dressed overall for the arrival of Queen Victoria; amid huge rejoicing, she dedicated the Forest 'for the use and enjoyment of my people for all time'. Nearby was (and still is) Queen Elizabeth I's hunting lodge.

Epping Forest is served by the Underground's Central Line, which has a loop running off to Chigwell. This village may be just the wrong side of the East London border, but it too is part of London's recreation area. In the churchyard we can find George Shillibeer; with his pioneering horsebus, he became the founder of London's bus service. Opposite is the King's Head, known to Charles Dickens, and Chigwell Hall, where the Metropolitan Police maintain their sports ground. The photographs suggest that today Dickens could easily find his way around. Chigwell was one of many East London villages which fed the capital. In the steam days, before the railway line became part of the Underground, a milk train would stop between Grange Hill and Chigwell Stations to load fruit and vegetables grown on the railway company's own farm for Liverpool Street Station's Great Eastern Hotel. Today the Underground's relatively new Victoria Line makes access to nearby Walthamstow even easier than when the Great Eastern Railway pushed out from Liverpool Street in Queen Victoria's reign.

East London is rich in history and architectural heritage which has yet to be properly recognised. Even the standard Pevsner 'Buildings of England' architectural reference series still lacks its long-promised East London volume. The Frith pictures in this book will not only stir memories, but also provide an invaluable basis for a record of how East London looked during the years of its greatest transformation.

The Tower and Tower Bridge

The Opening of Tower Bridge 1894 L130019
Tower Bridge was opened by the Prince of Wales in 1894; it was raised more than 6,000 times during its first year. The high-level footbridge was for pedestrians to use when the bridge was raised for ships to pass through. Today, the only resident is a cat to keep the mice away.

The Tower of London c1890 L130172
The Tower of London's now familiar look dates from the 19th century. The moat was drained in the 1840s, and the Waterloo Barracks, behind the central White Tower, was completed in 1850. The curtain defence, or inner wall, was newly reconstructed in the 1890s.

The Tower of London c1920 L130251
Eleven German spies were shot within the Tower of London during the First World War just before this photograph was taken, from a building in Trinity Square. In the foreground is Tower Hill, which falls within the Liberty of the Tower.

The Tower of London c1955 L1305022
It is high tide in the Pool of London in the summer, with the water lapping at the Tower of London's Traitors Gate. The view is taken from Tower Bridge, at a time when the Tower's backdrop was still free of the City of London's high buildings.

Tower Hamlets

Whitechapel Road 1885 L130214
The famous Victorian street market was one of London's largest; many of the traders were Jewish and Irish. On the knife sharpener's stall there are bunches of keys. It was said that you could buy anything for a house or garden in the market.

East Ham Barking Road c1965
E100002
This picture was taken within minutes of the other one. It now shows the view east, with more shops visible. Between 1881 and 1911 this area had one of the greatest increases in population; on each side of the main road there were rows of small houses for dockers.

East Ham, Barking Road c1965 E100001
This is the view enjoyed by a car driver in the 60s, travelling west from Barking towards central London and reaching the slight double bend at East Ham. On the left is Ranelagh Road. Bedford Road is to the right.

East Ham The Hammers c1965
E100004
The sign above the Watney's pub shows football players. The Hammers is the popular name for East Ham's football club. It started life in 1900 as the works football club of the nearby Thames Ironworks and Shipbuilding Company, where the workers were riveters using hammers.

Barking, East Street c1955 B440017
East Street, leading to the Barking Abbey site, is now a pedestrian area called Station Parade, and is often filled with market stalls. Set back on the left is the Magistrates' Court, which was built in 1893. Boots has moved to the left out of the picture.

Barking (South)

Barking
The Church c1955
B440019
St Margaret's dates from the 13th century, and survived when the more famous Barking Abbey alongside was pulled down. Today Barking's Abbey site, near the handy River Roding, forms a conservation area. The expression 'barking mad' is derived from the medieval asylum here.

Barking
East Street c1955
B440057
The photographer is standing on the rising road over the railway outside Barking Station. The street ahead is today a pedestrian area; traffic is routed to the right down the widened Cambridge Road at the side of Lloyd's Bank.

◄ **Barking, Ripple Road c1960** B440018
Ripple Road began at the junction with Barking's East Street. Today, this stretch is traffic-free. Beyond the bus stop on the right is the Police Station. The semi-circular window on the left has gone, but it is echoed by several windows in the new Vicarage Field shopping centre which replaces the buildings.

Barking, East Street c1965 B440079
Shop frontages in East Street, such as Killwick's and Boots, have been modernised in a decade, which has also seen the trolley buses and their overhead wires disappear.

Barking, Blakes Corner c1960 B440016
This, the East Street cross-roads, is the shopping centre of Barking; the overhead trolley-bus wires are still here at this date. The photographer is standing in the middle of the road, which has that once-familiar concrete surface; the view looks ahead into Ripple Road.

Barking Blakes Corner 1968
B440078
The street furniture and road surface have changed in just a few years. The trolley-bus wires have gone, but new fencing protects shoppers against the increasing traffic. Today, there is a bandstand in the centre of this now traffic-free area. But Barclays bank is still a landmark.

Barking
Longbridge Road c1955 B440014

Richard Widmark is starring in the film 'No Way Out' at the Odeon in Longbridge Road, the northern approach road to Barking Station. Although the cinema has closed today, the distinctive building remains, following its restoration.

Barking, Longbridge Road c1955 B440010
The six-wheel red trolley-buses on route 693 have stopped at the handy trolley stop outside the Odeon. Passengers also alighted here for Barking Station, which is just out of view across the road.

Barking, Longbridge Road c1960 B440050
This view was taken further down Longbridge Road beyond the Odeon. Today, the continuous line of shops and buildings on the left is broken by the Fanshaw Avenue roundabout. Here a trolley bus turns out of what is now a major junction.

P.C. WOOD & SON
OXO
OXO

Havering

Dagenham, Church Street c1955 D178004
The shops are thriving here in the historic heart of Dagenham - this was before the Dagenham Heathway shopping centre by one of the Underground stations became the focal point. Today the shops survive, but the buildings to the right have changed.

▼ **Dagenham, The Old Church c1960** D178036
Dagenham was a village built on dry ground between Thames-side marshland to the south and Hainault Forest to the north. Dagenham's old village church of St Peter and St Paul has a 13th-century chancel and lancet windows. The Cross Keys pub on the left is a 15th-century timber-framed hall house.

▼ **Dagenham, Interior View of The Ford Motor Works c1955** D178009
The Ford Motor Company purchased the land in 1924 and began production at Dagenham in 1931. The works, to the south of the old village, have spread on to the marshland and riverside to embrace an expanse of water known as Dagenham Reach.

▲ **Dagenham, The Ford Jetty and the River Thames c1955** D178012
The Ford Motor Company jetty is on Halfway Reach; this is named after a building which stood on the river bend opposite into the beginning of the 19th century. Opposite now is Crossness Sewerage Works on Erith Marshes.

◄ **Dagenham c1955** D178017
Timothy Whites & Taylors, the chemist, is two doors from the bank. The road ahead is Chequers Lane, which runs through Ford Motor Works. Today, with the decline of car manufacture, the shops and bank have gone, and the A13 through traffic has been diverted.

Rainham, Upminster Road c1950 R354002
In the 1950s, Rainham was still in Essex rather than in Greater London, and these shops and houses next to the churchyard are typical Essex weatherboarded buildings. The row survives, but the buildings have been altered.

Rainham, The Church c1960 R354036
The church of St Helen and St Giles is a rare example of a late Norman church, and the oldest building in Rainham. The large chancel roof is 15th-century. Rainham Hall, next to the church and in the care of the National Trust, was built in about 1729 by a sea captain who owned Rainham Wharf.

Rainham The Broadway c1955 R354011
A London Transport bus waits near the cafe in Rainham village centre, which is by the church and the railway station. The clock tower on the roundabout is Rainham's war memorial.

▼ **Rainham, Upminster Road c1960** R354024
This modern parade of shops was built only a few yards from the small old shops alongside the churchyard to meet the needs of the new residents, many of whom worked at nearby Fords in Dagenham.

▼ **Rainham, Upminster Road c1955** R354023
Planners looked to the future by moving the building line back for the new shops. Traffic is still light in this residential and shopping street, and there is a bus stop. A traditional pram is left outside a window, and a child plays in the street.

▲ **Rainham Upminster Road c1960** R354022
A sports shop, a dry cleaners and a bakers advertising slimming bread are among the shops in this old parade of shops. A Nurdin & Peacock lorry has arrived from Willesden with new supplies.

Rainham
The River c1960 R354034
Rainham Creek, the mouth of the Ingrebourne River, was the entrance to a port until the 19th century. Now, flood defences have turned the confluence with the River Thames into a pipeline. Meanwhile, Rainham Marshes, a medieval marshland on the eastern side, is preserved as a wildlife reserve.

◄ **Hornchurch**
The Village 1908 59856
The Britannia Inn, on the corner of the High Street and North Street, dated from at least the 15th century. It may have been a priory hostel for pilgrims travelling south to Canterbury by way of Brentford and a Thames ferry. The pub was demolished in 1938 to make way for Burton's.

◀ **Hornchurch**
St Andrew's Church 1908
59858

Hornchurch's large church stands on the site of a priory built in 1159 by Henry II and inhabited by monks from Savoy. Hornchurch means 'horned church'; this may refer to the bull's head and horns at the church's east end. St Andrew's, a large church when Hornchurch was just a village, has a 13th-century chancel.

◀ **Hornchurch**
The Village 1908 59855

This view shows the Hornchurch High Street junction with North Street to the left. Drake's, on the left, is a hairdresser and newsagent, whilst Franklyn's is a 'boot maker established in 1819'.

◄ **Hornchurch, High Street 1909** 62081
At the beginning of the 20th century, Hornchurch High Street still had the feel of an Essex village street, with most of the buildings being weatherboarded. The photographer is looking west towards London. On the right is the Bull, advertising local Romford Inde Coope ales.

▲ **Hornchurch, North Street 1909** 62082
The Church House on the right was a school for infants and girls; it was built in 1855 on land bought by New College, Oxford. The Baptist church opposite opened in 1882. Today, the school building survives - so does its original decorative iron railing, which is unusual. The Baptist church has been rebuilt on the corner of Leather Lane.

▼ **Hornchurch, High Street c1955** H115025
Half a century after the 1909 photograph was taken, the arrival of the car has robbed the High Street of its village atmosphere. The Odeon ahead is now Mecca Bingo, and the Bull has become the Fatling & Firkin. Sainsbury's is next door.

▼ **Hornchurch, High Street c1955** H115003
This picture shows the old protruding buildings just before they were removed to make way for more traffic and shoppers. The Little Flower Shop and its neighbours have been rebuilt. The house on the left, by the bus, is the bakers, an 18th-century building with a bow window, which was demolished in 1956.

▲ **Hornchurch**
The Windmill 1909
62085
Hornchurch windmill, which stood just south-east of the church, was working until 1912. There had been a mill on the site from about the 14th century; this last one was destroyed by fire in 1921.

◀ **Hornchurch**
The Cottage Homes 1908
60672

Boys and girls from Shoreditch living in the Hornchurch Cottage Homes were taught trades and domestic science. There was also military band training for the boys, who often went into the services. The site was sold for development in 1984, and the restored houses have been incorporated into the St Leonard's Hamlet housing estate.

◄ **Hornchurch Emerson Park Parkstone Avenue 1909** 62088

Parkstone Avenue takes its name from Parkstone in Poole, which was the home of the developer, William Carter. At the end of the 19th century, he bought 200 acres; by the time this picture was taken, there were 200 houses built near Emerson Park Station.

◄ **Hornchurch, Cottage Homes 1908** 60673
Hornchurch Cottage Homes were opened in 1889 by the Guardians of Shoreditch St Leonard's Poor Law Union, which had bought Harrow Lodge Farm opposite the Harrow pub. It was intended that 'the homeless would be brought up without the fear of, and away from, the shadow of the workhouse'. The sculpture came from Shoreditch.

▼ **Hornchurch, Great Nelmes Estate, Elm Grove 1909** 62089
Elm Grove runs north-south, and like its northern continuation Nelmes Way, it is mostly lined with chestnut trees. Conkers cover the ground of the now residential avenue in the autumn.

◄ **Hornchurch Emerson Park Berther Road 1909** 62086
Berther Road, which runs off the main road by Emerson Park Station, was one of the first to be developed by William Carter, so the houses had well-established gardens in 1909. Today, the corner house has lost its creeper and hedge, and the conservatory has been replaced with a modern version.

◄ **Upminster 1908** 60619
This 18th-century building survives, but it is now flanked by newer houses; it stands in Corbets Tey Road. To the right is Little Gaynes Lane. Although the house on the left still has creeper on its walls, the post box has gone and the area is less green.

Upminster, Bird Lane Corner 1909
62095
This family is standing in Hall Lane, to the north of Upminster. This area is known as Pot Kilns: the brick and tile industry had been situated here from 1708, and was to remain until 1930. Clay was dug out from both sides of Bird Lane on the left.

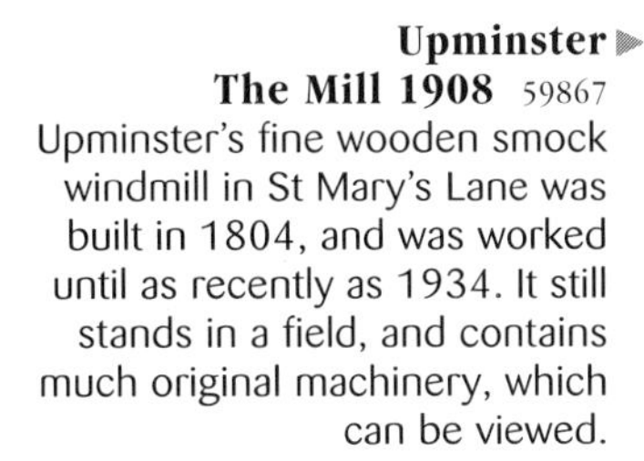

Upminster
The Mill 1908 59867
Upminster's fine wooden smock windmill in St Mary's Lane was built in 1804, and was worked until as recently as 1934. It still stands in a field, and contains much original machinery, which can be viewed.

Upminster, Deyncourt Gardens 1909 62090
This view looks west up Deyncourt Gardens from the junction with Courtenay Gardens on the right. Ahead, up the gentle slope, is a now-demolished house in Hall Lane. The corner house remains, but now has rural-style gates.

◄ **Upminster Waldegrave Gardens 1908** 59863

The cart advertises that it can deliver 'home killed meat'. The white fences have gone, and the entrance to the road has been rebuilt, but the houses in this picture remain, now with mature trees and hedges. Today the decorative ridge tiles on the roof line have given way to a satellite dish.

▼ **Upminster Courtenay Gardens 1909** 62091

This residential street was handy for the nearby Upminster Station, which could be reached in five minutes. The houses today are little changed except for the loss of the odd chimney, a rebuilt porch or two and new fencing and mature trees.

◄ **Upminster Upminster Court 1909** 62093

The neo-Georgian house, designed by local resident Sir Charles Reilly for the company director Arthur Williams, is seen here a year after it was completed. Later it became offices, and in the Second World War it was a refugee centre.

Upminster, Upminster Court 1909 62092

Today, this mansion is an annex to Enfield's Capel Manor College; its Schools of Horticulture, Floristry and Arboriculture are based here. This frontage is unchanged - but now, visitors passing under the portico will be prospective students enrolling on a course.

Upminster, Upminster Hill 1908 59861

This is the view looking west towards Hornchurch on the London road; at the bottom of the hill it crosses the Ingrebourne River. Behind the photographer is the windmill, which survives, but the houses in the picture have been replaced. Hornchurch's church spire appears to be almost lost in trees.

Upminster The Town Centre c1965 U9044

The tree on the left is part of the churchyard, which helps to retain the unchanging feel of this junction. This cross-roads in the centre of Upminster today has fenced crossings at the traffic lights to protect pedestrians from the increased traffic; Burton's has given way to Pizza Express.

Upminster
The Broadway 1908 60613
The Bell, on the corner of Corbets Tey Road and St Mary's Lane, faced the churchyard. The quiet cross-roads, with just a coal merchant's cart stopped at the inn, would have been typical at the time; Upminster used to be a quiet Essex town until the growth of motor traffic.

SEARSON BROS
H.TALBOT

Upminster
The Market 1908

60612

This row of shops is opposite the URC church in Station Road. Talbot's, the greengrocer and fruiterer, has today given way to a video shop, but the shop to the left now sells fruit and vegetables. Searson Brothers was a 'boot & shoe emporium'. The now-demolished Clock House is beyond, near the cross-roads.

Upminster, Corbets Tey Road c1965 U9084
Upminster's main shopping parade is opposite Upminster Park and south of the cross-roads. The shops in the picture have changed over the years, and today the bus stop has a shelter. The concrete road surface has worn well and largely remains.

Upminster, Upminster Common 1909 62096
Upminster Common is on the east side of the River Ingrebourne, which we can see here, and nearer Harold Wood to the north than to Upminster village. This is typical Essex countryside; it was then considered to be far from London, and was known to the First World War poet Edward Thomas.

Corbets Tey
The Village 1908 60618
Corbets Tey is a conservation area just south of Upminster; it is now joined to it by continuous housing. These typical weatherboarded Essex cottages still survive in Harwood Hall Lane. The old village, on a tributary of the Ingrebourne River, has several 17th- and 18th-century buildings.

CARTER'S
DAREN

◄ **Ardleigh Green**
Ardleigh Green Road c1955 A301005
The parade of shops at the north end of Ardleigh Green Road has today become even more of a focus, with the two on the right becoming a one-stop shop. The corner cottage with the rounded doorway is now a cafe.

▲ **Ardleigh Green**
The Village 1955 A301007
Here we see the newsagents at Ardleigh Green, with an old-fashioned pram and a lady's bicycle outside. The road ahead is Squirrels Heath Lane, and the shops are on the corner leading into Ardleigh Green Road.

Ardleigh Green, Squirrels Heath Lane c1955 A301002
This view is looking east along Squirrels Heath Lane towards Ardleigh Green. The turning on the left is Ashlyn Grove, and Kingsley Gardens is by the lamp post on the right.

Ardleigh Green, The Cross Roads c1955 A301012
This is the peaceful view looking east from the end of Ardleigh Green Road at the cross-roads with the Southend Arterial Road. In the 50s, when there was much less traffic, the Esso slogan was 'happy motoring'. Today the petrol station is a Kwik-Fit garage.

Gidea Park
Hare Street c1955 G270002
Gidea Park is the 20th-century eastern extension of Romford. Today Hare Street, part of a Roman Road to Colchester, is known as Main Road. Ahead is the Arts and Crafts design shopping parade.

Gidea Park
Hare Street c1955 G270008

The building on the corner of Gidea Park's Main Road and Balgores Lane was built during the First World War; it is an example of the Arts and Crafts buildings which made up Romford's garden suburb.

Romford
The Market 1910 62770
Romford Market received its charter from Henry III in 1247. Henry IV gave permission for a wood to be cleared for St Edward the Confessor Church. The present building with its tall spire was erected in 1850; it was built in 14th-century style. Inside are monuments dating back to Elizabeth I's reign.

THE GLOBE
INN.

Romford
The Market 1908

59811

The Cock & Bell Inn on the left, next to Romford Church, was built in the 1480 as Church House; it housed a priest who served the chantry of Henry VII's Treasurer in the old church. The house was an inn during the 19th century to meet the needs of the huge coach trade on the London road.

◄ **Romford**
The Market c1950
R52031
The brewery off the High Street can be seen above the buildings on the left. There are cattle in the right-hand corner. Today the market is open on Wednesdays, Fridays and Saturdays; it sells food, household goods and clothes, and remains at least as large as it was in the early 20th century.

Romford
The Market 1908

59812

Here we have another view of the Cock & Bell Inn, which is next to the parish church and two doors from J E Castle Commercial Printers. On the central island pavement is a handy open-air toilet lit by a lamp post.

Romford
The Market Place c1950 R52030

At this time the market still had a clear through road for traffic using the High Street, which meant it was necessary to have a police officer at the Golden Lion cross-roads on market days. The Midland Bank on the north side near the church remains, but now calls itself HSBC.

Romford
Laurie Square 1908

59818

Laurie Square, intended as part of a larger development at the east end of the town, was built in the mid 19th century, and was contemporary with similar Victorian housing schemes in Kensington. The square has now disappeared to make way for the public library. The church tower belongs to St Edward's Roman Catholic Church.

Romford, The Railway Station 1908 59826
Romford railway station retained its rural charm until 1930; then, the Romford Railway Improvement Scheme enlarged the buildings to accommodate the growing numbers of commuters. The milk churns are a reminder of how Romford still fed the capital from its farmland and glasshouses.

K
BOOTS
THOMAS WALLIS & Co
STATION
RCUS, LONDON

Romford, The Brewery 1908 59827A
The River Rom flows through the Romford Brewery, where most of the buildings were already almost a century old in 1908. Edward Ind bought a pub which brewed beer in 1799. In 1845 he joined up with the brothers George and Octavius Coope to form Ind Coope. Production ceased in 1993, and the site has now been redeveloped.

Romford, Junction Road 1908 59819
In 1908, Junction Road would have been considered to be on the eastern edge of Romford. It is now a town centre residential road. The wooden fences have not survived, but the trees on the left remain as mature specimens.

Romford
Como Street 1908 59816
At first, Como Street just ran from North Street for a few yards to the River Rom. The housing terraces were built after 1883, with each block being given a name. This picture is taken from the junction with Olive Street, looking east towards the bridge over the River Rom.

DRAPER
TEL.
THE
FRUIT

Romford
South Street 1908

59808

South Street, linking the station with the market, was Romford's growing shopping street during the early 20th century. On the left is Barten's, a draper's, and next door is Rand, 'the Romford fruit stores'. Further ahead on the opposite side there are decorators' ladders to be seen. Just visible at the far end is the Golden Lion.

AND RETAIL
W. BARROW.
MERCHANT
JUBILEE
COFFEE
TAVERN
FRANK J DOLLEY

Romford, High Street 1908 59807
This picture may have been taken on a Sunday or after a special occasion. The High Street is not crowded, and the children are neatly dressed. The view east shows Frank Dulley's premises, which offered picture framing, plumbing, keys and glassware. Frank Dulley opposite is also a plumber.

Noak Hill
St Thomas's Church and the School 1908 59852
Noak Hill means 'hill by the oak tree'. The red brick church was built over two years, and was completed in 1842. The design is by Edward Blore, architect to William IV, who had been on the throne for two years when the church opened.

Collier Row
The Church and the Village 1908 59843
Collier Row means 'charcoal-burners' dwellings', which were here when this was a densely wooded area on the edge of Epping Forest. In the early 19th century, old cottages around the junction of Old Shoe Lane and Collier Row Lane were the main buildings.

Barking (North)

Dagenham
The Civic Centre, Beacontree Heath c1955 D178003
Dagenham's Civic Centre, designed by E Barry Webber, was built on Beacontree Heath and opened in 1937. At this time, the population was growing quickly, and the Becontree Estate was being developed; it was built by the London County Council on four square miles of flat land to the south.

Redbridge

Seven Kings
High Street c1955 S639006
Seven Kings is derived from 'Sevekyngges', which was its name in 1285. Claims that this was the meeting place of seven Saxon kings have never been confirmed. This eastern extension of Iford had London Transport trolley-buses in the 1950s.

Ilford, High Road c1960 134022
We are looking east down Ilford High Road; by this time the Town Hall is already masked by a new building. Beyond the Clements Road turning on the right, the High Road is a pedestrian-only shopping street.

Ilford, The Town Hall c1960 134024
Ilford's distinctive Town Hall, on the corner of Oakfield Road and the High Road, was known as the Oriental Town Hall when it opened in 1901. The shopping street in front is now traffic-free.

Ilford, Cranbrook Road c1965 134030
This view is looking north from outside Ilford Station. The road to the right, in front of C&A, is Ley Street, which has today disappeared to make way for the entrance to the Exchange shopping centre.

PUDDICOMBE
FURRIER
ANK
STOUT
ABC
HAINES & WARWICK
CRAVENA

Epping Forest

Leytonstone, High Road c1950 L374001
This view is looking down Leytonstone High Road from the corner of Grove Road. The pinnacle on the tower of St John's Church can be seen above the building beyond Barclay's Bank. The now-disappeared ABC cafe and the Maypole were familiar chains across the capital.

Leytonstone
St John's Church c1950 L374002
Leytonstone Church, dedicated to St John the Baptist, was built in 1832-3 on the corner of Church Lane. The design is by Edward Blore. There had been slight alterations by the 1950s. London Transport trolley-buses still ran past in High Road.

Snaresbrook
Eagle Pond 1903 50620B

Eagle Pond, on the edge of Epping Forest and once popular with fishermen, takes it name from the Eagle coaching inn nearby. This was an important stop on the London to Newmarket road, and into the 20th century was open for breakfast, luncheon and teas.

CHARRINGTON'S FINE ALE & NOTED STOUT
TO
GEORGE LANE
STATION
5 MINUTES

Woodford, High Road 1921 70105
The George on the left gave its name to George Lane, and, of course, to the station, which has become South Woodford Underground Station. Today the pub is built on the site of the early 18th-century Horns Inn; it is still covered in creeper at the front.

Woodford, George Lane 1921 70095
This view is looking up the street from a point above the level crossing at George Lane Station, which since 1937 has been called South Woodford. Today, the level crossing has gone, but the buildings ahead and on the right survive.

South Woodford, High Road c1965 S643018
Here we have a similar view of the George forty years after photograph No 70105; the carefree cyclists are now replaced by cars. Today, the Majestic cinema survives as simply the ABC, and the Vauxhall Rover car showroom is now adorned with just the Jaguar logo.

South Woodford, High Road c1965 S643006
The view was taken outside the George looking north, with George Lane to the right. Today, the pub has a better sign showing the figure of King George, and the shops remain. However, the white building on the far right has been demolished; and where the trees are, ahead, the North Circular and Southend Road pass underneath.

South Woodford
High Road c1965 S643009
The parade of shops is on the north side of the main road. Today, the chemist, on the corner of Chelmsford Road, has now celebrated its centenary, and has been rebuilt with an upper floor. Glovers has become the Post Office.

Woodford Green
All Saints Church 1908 60265
The church was built in 1874 on part of the Monkhams Glade Estate to meet the growth of population drifting out from the capital. Today, there is still a wide expanse of green on the south side, and the house to the right survives.

Woodford Green, All Saints Church 1904 53061
This picture is a little earlier than the close-up view; it shows the church's important landmark role and rural setting. Clarendon House and Firtree Cottage are on the left. Warner's Path can be seen running through the grass on the right. Once cows grazed here, and wandered on to the main road.

Woodford, High Road 1903 50604
We are looking north up the street, with the Castle to the left; we can see the Wesleyan Church just before it was converted to a Men's Club. On the right is the London Joint Stock Bank.

Woodford High Road c1950
W131021
This view, similar to No 50604, was taken half a century later with cars replacing carts. The bank on the right has been rebuilt with a dome added, and has become the Midland; the Men's Club, the former church, has had its tower remodelled.

◄ **Woodford Green High Road c1950** W132019
This view looks south from the junction with John's Road, which leads down to Woodford Station. The Midland Bank dome can be seen on the left, but the number 20 bus, with its British European Airways advertisements, hides the Castle pub forecourt.

◄ **Woodford Green The Wilfred Lawson Temperance Hotel 1921** 70106

The temperance hotel, opened in 1883 by Sir Wilfred Lawson MP, was on the corner of Chingford Lane and the High Road. After the Second World War it became a nurses' training centre, before being demolished in 1974. The site is now occupied by the Churchill flats.

Woodford Green High Road c1950 W132017

This view was also taken from the St John's Road and High Road junction, but this time looking north with Johnson's Pond to the right. It was named after a butcher who traded opposite in the days when cattle grazed here; they were watered at the pond, which still has a pump.

Woodford Green, Harts Sanitorium 1921 70123

The house was the home of the botanist Richard Warner, who cultivated the first gardenia to flower in England, and studied the flora of Woodford. He also gave his name to the footpath running across the green near the church. The house and grounds are now a housing development.

Woodford Green Bancroft's School 1921 70119

This view of the school from the side road shows the High Road without its central reservation barrier, which today blocks the view. The Drapers' Company School moved here from the East End's Mile End Road in 1886; at that time, this new building replaced a former workhouse known as Hanover Lodge.

ESTATE AGENTS
DORIS DAY
PLAYER'S NAVY GUT TOBACCO.
DAYS
MXB 475

◄ **Woodford Bridge, High Road c1950** W479013
The thriving shops are seen here at a time when there were still no major supermarkets, and parking was easy for those who used a car from the many new houses nearby. A large poster advertises an appearance by the singer Doris Day.

▲ **Woodford Bridge, High Road c1950** W479015
The same shops are seen as by a traveller going north towards nearby Chigwell, where there were more shops. School children can be seen walking along the road passing the greengrocer's beyond Watkin's and the Post Office.

Woodford Bridge St Paul's Church 1908
60271
The attractive country church by the green only dates from 1854. This view shows the building, with its landmark spire, just twenty years after it was damaged by a serious fire. Behind is a view across the Roding Valley.

◄ **Woodford Bridge High Road c1965**
W479038
The same street is seen a decade later when the number of cars has increased. There has also been some tree felling. Changes to the buildings include the restoration of a blocked window just beyond the bus stop.

▼ **Woodford Bridge Dr Barnardo's Gwynne House 1921**
70156
The house was built in 1816. It takes its name from an earlier building on the site, where it is believed that Nell Gwynne, Charles II's famous actress mistress, lived. After Dr Barnardo's sold the house, it became the Prince Regent Hotel.

◄ **Woodford Bridge Claybury Asylum 1908**
60271a
Claybury Hospital was a London County Council asylum built in the 1890s; it was deliberately sited on the rural edge of London in the grounds of Claybury Hall, which had been laid out a century earlier by Humphrey Repton. The grounds are now a housing development.

◄ **Chigwell Harsnetts 1925** 78721
At the top of the hill, just before the open-top car, is the King's Head. In Charles Dickens' 'Barnaby Rudge', this is called the Maypole, and described as 'an old building with more gable ends than a lazy man would care to count on a sunny day'.

Chigwell, St Mary's Church 1925 78728
St Mary's dates from the Norman period. In the churchyard is the tomb of George Shillibeer, founder of London buses. His horse-drawn service ran from Marylebone to the City in 1829. Also buried here is John Knight of Knight's Castile soap fame.

Chigwell Ye Olde King's Head Gardens 1925 78725
The garden of the King's Head was extremely popular in the years between the two world wars. The pub garden has changed now, although it is still popular in with visitors and nearby residents in the summer.

◄ **Chigwell**
The Village 1925 78724
The heart of the old village is on the High Road, immediately north-west of the historic church, the King's Head and the school; it is away from the station, which offered a new focal point for building.

◄ **Chigwell, The Grammar School 1925** 78726
Chigwell School was founded in 1629 by Samuel Harsnett, who had been vicar from 1597 until 1605 during the reigns of Elizabeth I and James I. Harsnett, who knew and inspired Shakespeare when he was writing 'King Lear', became Archbishop of York in the same year that the school opened. An early pupil was William Penn, who founded Pennsylvania.

▼ **Chigwell The Village c1955** C88006
A bakery serving teas attracted visitors who could arrive by a London bus which stopped almost outside. The simple signpost at the top of the road is pointing down Vicarage Lane, which leads to Grange Hill.

◄ **Chigwell, Chigwell Hall c1955** C88053
Chigwell Hall and its parkland is now the Metropolitan Police Sports Ground. The building, the former manor house, owes its landmark chimneys to the architect Norman Shaw, who redesigned the house in 1876. This is his only building in Essex - the village is still officially just outside Greater London.

Chigwell
The Golf Club c1955

C88050

Golf is a popular pastime in Essex, and especially here in the green belt, where there are numerous well-established sports fields. Chigwell Golf Course was created handily near the railway station.

Chigwell, Brook Parade c1950 C88009
This parade of shops is to the south of the old village centre across the valley of the Chigwell Brook. The photograph is taken from the corner of Station Road. The railway reached here in 1903, and became part of the Underground's Central Line in 1948.

Chigwell The Swimming Pool Grange Farm Centre c1955 C88022
On an obviously very hot day, it is not so much the architecture of the pool and its surroundings which date the picture, but the casual clothes of the spectators and the swimwear.

Chigwell Home Farm c1960 C88108
Here we have a rural scene at Home Farm to the north-west of Chigwell village, which has remarkable unspoilt farmland within walking distance of the Underground station. The 1950s and early 1960s were tranquil years before the intrusive sound of the M11 began to drift over the land.

Chingford
The Old Church 1906

55338

When this photograph was taken, it was just two years since the nave roof had fallen in. The last service was held in 1889, but the church was well-known owing to Arthur Hughes' painting 'Home from the Sea', which showed the view similar to this photograph. More than twenty years were to pass before the decaying building was restored.

Chingford, Queen Elizabeth's Hunting Lodge 1903 50614
The unique Queen Elizabeth's Hunting Lodge was built in 1543, before Elizabeth's reign. The galleries were originally open, so that the hunting party could view or even shoot at deer driven towards them. Elizabeth I is said to have ridden her horse up the stairs to celebrate the defeat of the Spanish Armada in 1588.

Chingford, The Royal Forest Hotel 1903 50613
The Royal Forest Hotel, next to Queen Elizabeth's Hunting Lodge, was first built in 1880. After a serious fire in 1912, there were changes in the 1930s; but the hotel remained popular, and the coach house was adapted for the motor car.

Chingford The Railway Station 1882 C95301
In May 1882, a ceremonial arch was built outside Chingford Station to welcome Queen Victoria, who came for a ceremony at High Beach. Epping Forest had just been saved from development, and the Queen declared: 'It gives me the greatest satisfaction to dedicate this beautiful Forest to the use and enjoyment of my people for all time'.

Chingford, Connaught Water 1904 53056
Connaught Water, in Epping Forest and near Chingford, is an artificial lake dug in the 19th century and named after Queen Victoria's son, the Duke of Connaught. In 1882 he was appointed as the first Ranger after the Corporation of London had purchased the Forest, which was known as 'London's back garden'.

◀ **Highams Park**
Boats and the Landing Stage 1921 70115
Highams Park, near Woodford Green, is the remains of the Manor of Hecham (meaning 'high home') and part of Epping Forest. In 1793 Humphry Repton was employed to landscape the Higham House grounds and to create the lake from the River Ching.

▲ **Highams Park, The Lake 1921** 70114
The lake was a popular place for weekend and holiday recreation; this was made possible in 1891, when the Corporation of London, which had already saved the adjacent Epping Forest from development, bought thirty acres, including the lake.

F&Co
TAILORS
EVERETT BROS
PRINTERS
BOOKBINDERS
EVERETT

Walthamstow High Street 1904

51421

The scene is very quiet for a street which not only had a market, but clearly numerous businesses, including a printers. On the right are a stationers, a toy shop and a tailors, who claim to be 'the only up to date tailors for working men'. Opposite is a Hackney Empire hoarding.

Walthamstow
The Church 1904
53053
An adult and two children are watching the photographer and standing still during the long exposure - unlike the stray figure on the right. Inside, the church monuments include one to the draper Sir George Monoux; he became Lord Mayor of London in 1514, and founded the nearby almshouses.

◄ **Walthamstow St Mary's Church 1903** 50602

The large notice warns: 'cyclists not allowed to ride through churchyard'. St Mary's was founded in the 12th century by the family of William I's standard bearer, Ralph de Toni. Although the church has been rebuilt, the tower and chancel chapels date from 1535.

▼ **Walthamstow Upper Walthamstow Road 1906** 55208

Already well established at the turn of the century, Upper Walthamstow Road was handy for both Wood Street Station at the west end and the fringes of Epping Forest at the other.

◄ **Walthamstow St James Street 1906** 55200

The parish of St James, at the west end of Walthamstow's High Street, was created as the town expanded in the 19th century. The Great Eastern Railway's St James Street station was a vital link with London, as the Underground did not arrive here until 1968.

M. TINSON.
SURGERY.
SURGERY.
WOOD STREET STAT
EASTERN RAILW
HIGHAMS-PARK & CHINGFOR

Walthamstow, Wood Street 1907 58548B
The station is in Upper Walthamstow, near Epping Forest, which just 30 years before this picture was taken had been saved from development. This was an early commuter suburb: steam trains ran not only north from here up the Forest to Chingford, but also south-west to Liverpool Street in the City.

Walthamstow, Lloyd Park 1904 51426

The park embraces Water House, which had been the childhood home of the artist and designer William Morris from 1848 to 1856. Walthamstow was then still in Essex countryside, and was cut off from Greater London by the River Lea. Today the house is a Morris museum.

Walthamstow, Lloyd Park 1906 55198

Index

Frith Book Co Titles

www.francisfrith.co.uk

The Frith Book Company publishes over 100 new titles each year. A selection of those currently available are listed below. For latest catalogue please contact Frith Book Co.

Town Books 96 pages, approx 100 photos. County and Themed Books 128 pages, approx 150 photos (unless specified). All titles hardback laminated case and jacket except those indicated pb (paperback)

Title	ISBN	Price
Amersham, Chesham & Rickmansworth (pb)	1-85937-340-2	£9.99
Ancient Monuments & Stone Circles	1-85937-143-4	£17.99
Aylesbury (pb)	1-85937-227-9	£9.99
Bakewell	1-85937-113-2	£12.99
Barnstaple (pb)	1-85937-300-3	£9.99
Bath (pb)	1-85937-419-0	£9.99
Bedford (pb)	1-85937-205-8	£9.99
Berkshire (pb)	1-85937-191-4	£9.99
Berkshire Churches	1-85937-170-1	£17.99
Blackpool (pb)	1-85937-382-8	£9.99
Bognor Regis (pb)	1-85937-431-x	£9.99
Bournemouth	1-85937-067-5	£12.99
Bradford (pb)	1-85937-204-x	£9.99
Brighton & Hove(pb)	1-85937-192-2	£8.99
Bristol (pb)	1-85937-264-3	£9.99
British Life A Century Ago (pb)	1-85937-213-9	£9.99
Buckinghamshire (pb)	1-85937-200-7	£9.99
Camberley (pb)	1-85937-222-8	£9.99
Cambridge (pb)	1-85937-422-0	£9.99
Cambridgeshire (pb)	1-85937-420-4	£9.99
Canals & Waterways (pb)	1-85937-291-0	£9.99
Canterbury Cathedral (pb)	1-85937-179-5	£9.99
Cardiff (pb)	1-85937-093-4	£9.99
Carmarthenshire	1-85937-216-3	£14.99
Chelmsford (pb)	1-85937-310-0	£9.99
Cheltenham (pb)	1-85937-095-0	£9.99
Cheshire (pb)	1-85937-271-6	£9.99
Chester	1-85937-090-x	£12.99
Chesterfield	1-85937-378-x	£9.99
Chichester (pb)	1-85937-228-7	£9.99
Colchester (pb)	1-85937-188-4	£8.99
Cornish Coast	1-85937-163-9	£14.99
Cornwall (pb)	1-85937-229-5	£9.99
Cornwall Living Memories	1-85937-248-1	£14.99
Cotswolds (pb)	1-85937-230-9	£9.99
Cotswolds Living Memories	1-85937-255-4	£14.99
County Durham	1-85937-123-x	£14.99
Croydon Living Memories	1-85937-162-0	£9.99
Cumbria	1-85937-101-9	£14.99
Dartmoor	1-85937-145-0	£14.99
Derby (pb)	1-85937-367-4	£9.99
Derbyshire (pb)	1-85937-196-5	£9.99
Devon (pb)	1-85937-297-x	£9.99
Dorset (pb)	1-85937-269-4	£9.99
Dorset Churches	1-85937-172-8	£17.99
Dorset Coast (pb)	1-85937-299-6	£9.99
Dorset Living Memories	1-85937-210-4	£14.99
Down the Severn	1-85937-118-3	£14.99
Down the Thames (pb)	1-85937-278-3	£9.99
Down the Trent	1-85937-311-9	£14.99
Dublin (pb)	1-85937-231-7	£9.99
East Anglia (pb)	1-85937-265-1	£9.99
East London	1-85937-080-2	£14.99
East Sussex	1-85937-130-2	£14.99
Eastbourne	1-85937-061-6	£12.99
Edinburgh (pb)	1-85937-193-0	£8.99
England in the 1880s	1-85937-331-3	£17.99
English Castles (pb)	1-85937-434-4	£9.99
English Country Houses	1-85937-161-2	£17.99
Essex (pb)	1-85937-270-8	£9.99
Exeter	1-85937-126-4	£12.99
Exmoor	1-85937-132-9	£14.99
Falmouth	1-85937-066-7	£12.99
Folkestone (pb)	1-85937-124-8	£9.99
Glasgow (pb)	1-85937-190-6	£9.99
Gloucestershire	1-85937-102-7	£14.99
Great Yarmouth (pb)	1-85937-426-3	£9.99
Greater Manchester (pb)	1-85937-266-x	£9.99
Guildford (pb)	1-85937-410-7	£9.99
Hampshire (pb)	1-85937-279-1	£9.99
Hampshire Churches (pb)	1-85937-207-4	£9.99
Harrogate	1-85937-423-9	£9.99
Hastings & Bexhill (pb)	1-85937-131-0	£9.99
Heart of Lancashire (pb)	1-85937-197-3	£9.99
Helston (pb)	1-85937-214-7	£9.99
Hereford (pb)	1-85937-175-2	£9.99
Herefordshire	1-85937-174-4	£14.99
Hertfordshire (pb)	1-85937-247-3	£9.99
Horsham (pb)	1-85937-432-8	£9.99
Humberside	1-85937-215-5	£14.99
Hythe, Romney Marsh & Ashford	1-85937-256-2	£9.99

Available from your local bookshop or from the publisher

Frith Book Co Titles (continued)

Title	ISBN	Price
Ipswich (pb)	1-85937-424-7	£9.99
Ireland (pb)	1-85937-181-7	£9.99
Isle of Man (pb)	1-85937-268-6	£9.99
Isles of Scilly	1-85937-136-1	£14.99
Isle of Wight (pb)	1-85937-429-8	£9.99
Isle of Wight Living Memories	1-85937-304-6	£14.99
Kent (pb)	1-85937-189-2	£9.99
Kent Living Memories	1-85937-125-6	£14.99
Lake District (pb)	1-85937-275-9	£9.99
Lancaster, Morecambe & Heysham (pb)	1-85937-233-3	£9.99
Leeds (pb)	1-85937-202-3	£9.99
Leicester	1-85937-073-x	£12.99
Leicestershire (pb)	1-85937-185-x	£9.99
Lincolnshire (pb)	1-85937-433-6	£9.99
Liverpool & Merseyside (pb)	1-85937-234-1	£9.99
London (pb)	1-85937-183-3	£9.99
Ludlow (pb)	1-85937-176-0	£9.99
Luton (pb)	1-85937-235-x	£9.99
Maidstone	1-85937-056-x	£14.99
Manchester (pb)	1-85937-198-1	£9.99
Middlesex	1-85937-158-2	£14.99
New Forest	1-85937-128-0	£14.99
Newark (pb)	1-85937-366-6	£9.99
Newport, Wales (pb)	1-85937-258-9	£9.99
Newquay (pb)	1-85937-421-2	£9.99
Norfolk (pb)	1-85937-195-7	£9.99
Norfolk Living Memories	1-85937-217-1	£14.99
Northamptonshire	1-85937-150-7	£14.99
Northumberland Tyne & Wear (pb)	1-85937-281-3	£9.99
North Devon Coast	1-85937-146-9	£14.99
North Devon Living Memories	1-85937-261-9	£14.99
North London	1-85937-206-6	£14.99
North Wales (pb)	1-85937-298-8	£9.99
North Yorkshire (pb)	1-85937-236-8	£9.99
Norwich (pb)	1-85937-194-9	£8.99
Nottingham (pb)	1-85937-324-0	£9.99
Nottinghamshire (pb)	1-85937-187-6	£9.99
Oxford (pb)	1-85937-411-5	£9.99
Oxfordshire (pb)	1-85937-430-1	£9.99
Peak District (pb)	1-85937-280-5	£9.99
Penzance	1-85937-069-1	£12.99
Peterborough (pb)	1-85937-219-8	£9.99
Piers	1-85937-237-6	£17.99
Plymouth	1-85937-119-1	£12.99
Poole & Sandbanks (pb)	1-85937-251-1	£9.99
Preston (pb)	1-85937-212-0	£9.99
Reading (pb)	1-85937-238-4	£9.99
Romford (pb)	1-85937-319-4	£9.99
Salisbury (pb)	1-85937-239-2	£9.99
Scarborough (pb)	1-85937-379-8	£9.99
St Albans (pb)	1-85937-341-0	£9.99
St Ives (pb)	1-85937415-8	£9.99
Scotland (pb)	1-85937-182-5	£9.99
Scottish Castles (pb)	1-85937-323-2	£9.99
Sevenoaks & Tunbridge	1-85937-057-8	£12.99
Sheffield, South Yorks (pb)	1-85937-267-8	£9.99
Shrewsbury (pb)	1-85937-325-9	£9.99
Shropshire (pb)	1-85937-326-7	£9.99
Somerset	1-85937-153-1	£14.99
South Devon Coast	1-85937-107-8	£14.99
South Devon Living Memories	1-85937-168-x	£14.99
South Hams	1-85937-220-1	£14.99
Southampton (pb)	1-85937-427-1	£9.99
Southport (pb)	1-85937-425-5	£9.99
Staffordshire	1-85937-047-0	£12.99
Stratford upon Avon	1-85937-098-5	£12.99
Suffolk (pb)	1-85937-221-x	£9.99
Suffolk Coast	1-85937-259-7	£14.99
Surrey (pb)	1-85937-240-6	£9.99
Sussex (pb)	1-85937-184-1	£9.99
Swansea (pb)	1-85937-167-1	£9.99
Tees Valley & Cleveland	1-85937-211-2	£14.99
Thanet (pb)	1-85937-116-7	£9.99
Tiverton (pb)	1-85937-178-7	£9.99
Torbay	1-85937-063-2	£12.99
Truro	1-85937-147-7	£12.99
Victorian and Edwardian Cornwall	1-85937-252-x	£14.99
Victorian & Edwardian Devon	1-85937-253-8	£14.99
Victorian & Edwardian Kent	1-85937-149-3	£14.99
Vic & Ed Maritime Album	1-85937-144-2	£17.99
Victorian and Edwardian Sussex	1-85937-157-4	£14.99
Victorian & Edwardian Yorkshire	1-85937-154-x	£14.99
Victorian Seaside	1-85937-159-0	£17.99
Villages of Devon (pb)	1-85937-293-7	£9.99
Villages of Kent (pb)	1-85937-294-5	£9.99
Villages of Sussex (pb)	1-85937-295-3	£9.99
Warwickshire (pb)	1-85937-203-1	£9.99
Welsh Castles (pb)	1-85937-322-4	£9.99
West Midlands (pb)	1-85937-289-9	£9.99
West Sussex	1-85937-148-5	£14.99
West Yorkshire (pb)	1-85937-201-5	£9.99
Weymouth (pb)	1-85937-209-0	£9.99
Wiltshire (pb)	1-85937-277-5	£9.99
Wiltshire Churches (pb)	1-85937-171-x	£9.99
Wiltshire Living Memories	1-85937-245-7	£14.99
Winchester (pb)	1-85937-428-x	£9.99
Windmills & Watermills	1-85937-242-2	£17.99
Worcester (pb)	1-85937-165-5	£9.99
Worcestershire	1-85937-152-3	£14.99
York (pb)	1-85937-199-x	£9.99
Yorkshire (pb)	1-85937-186-8	£9.99
Yorkshire Living Memories	1-85937-166-3	£14.99

See Frith books on the internet www.francisfrith.co.uk

FRITH PRODUCTS & SERVICES

Francis Frith would doubtless be pleased to know that the pioneering publishing venture he started in 1860 still continues today. A hundred and forty years later, The Francis Frith Collection continues in the same innovative tradition and is now one of the foremost publishers of vintage photographs in the world. Some of the current activities include:

Interior Decoration

Today Frith's photographs can be seen framed and as giant wall murals in thousands of pubs, restaurants, hotels, banks, retail stores and other public buildings throughout the country. In every case they enhance the unique local atmosphere of the places they depict and provide reminders of gentler days in an increasingly busy and frenetic world.

Product Promotions

Frith products are used by many major companies to promote the sales of their own products or to reinforce their own history and heritage. Frith promotions have been used by Hovis bread, Courage beers, Scots Porage Oats, Colman's mustard, Cadbury's foods, Mellow Birds coffee, Dunhill pipe tobacco, Guinness, and Bulmer's Cider.

Genealogy and Family History

As the interest in family history and roots grows world-wide, more and more people are turning to Frith's photographs of Great Britain for images of the towns, villages and streets where their ancestors lived; and, of course, photographs of the churches and chapels where their ancestors were christened, married and buried are an essential part of every genealogy tree and family album.

Frith Products

All Frith photographs are available Framed or just as Mounted Prints and Posters (size 23 x 16 inches). These may be ordered from the address below. From time to time other products - Address Books, Calendars, Table Mats, etc - are available.

The Internet

Already twenty thousand Frith photographs can be viewed and purchased on the internet through the Frith websites and a myriad of partner sites.

For more detailed information on Frith companies and products, look at these sites:

www.francisfrith.co.uk
www.francisfrith.com
(for North American visitors)

See the complete list of Frith Books at:
www.francisfrith.co.uk
This web site is regularly updated with the latest list of publications from the Frith Book Company. If you wish to buy books relating to another part of the country that your local bookshop does not stock, you may purchase on-line.

For further information, trade, or author enquiries please contact us at the address below:
The Francis Frith Collection, Frith's Barn, Teffont, Salisbury, Wiltshire, England SP3 5QP.
Tel: +44 (0)1722 716 376 Fax: +44 (0)1722 716 881 Email: sales@francisfrith.co.uk

See Frith books on the internet www.francisfrith.co.uk

TO RECEIVE YOUR FREE MOUNTED PRINT

Mounted Print
Overall size 14 x 11 inches

Cut out this Voucher and return it with your remittance for £1.95 to cover postage and handling, to UK addresses. For overseas addresses please include £4.00 post and handling.
Choose any photograph included in this book. Your SEPIA print will be A4 in size, and mounted in a cream mount with burgundy rule line, overall size 14 x 11 inches.

Order additional Mounted Prints at HALF PRICE (only £7.49 each*)
If there are further pictures you would like to order, possibly as gifts for friends and family, purchase them at half price (no additional postage and handling required).

Have your Mounted Prints framed*
For an additional £14.95 per print you can have your chosen Mounted Print framed in an elegant polished wood and gilt moulding, overall size 16 x 13 inches (no additional postage and handling required).

*** IMPORTANT!**
These special prices are only available if ordered using the original voucher on this page (no copies permitted) and at the same time as your free Mounted Print, for delivery to the same address

Frith Collectors' Guild

From time to time we publish a magazine of news and stories about Frith photographs and further special offers of Frith products. If you would like 12 months FREE membership, please return this form.

Send completed forms to:
The Francis Frith Collection, Frith's Barn, Teffont, Salisbury, Wiltshire SP3 5QP

Voucher for **FREE** and Reduced Price Frith Prints

Picture no.	Page number	Qty	Mounted @ £7.49	Framed + £14.95	Total Cost
		1	**Free of charge***	£	£
			£7.49	£	£
			£7.49	£	£
			£7.49	£	£
			£7.49	£	£
			£7.49	£	£
Please allow 28 days for delivery			*** Post & handling**		**£1.95**
Book Title			**Total Order Cost**		**£**

Please do not photocopy this voucher. Only the original is valid, so please cut it out and return it to us.

I enclose a cheque / postal order for £ ....
made payable to 'The Francis Frith Collection'
OR please debit my Mastercard / Visa / Switch / Amex card
(credit cards please on all overseas orders)

Number ....

Issue No (Switch only) .... Valid from (Amex/Switch) ....

Expires .... Signature ....

Name Mr/Mrs/Ms ....

Address ....

....

....

.... Postcode ....

Daytime Tel No .... Valid to 31/12/02

The Francis Frith Collectors' Guild

Please enrol me as a member for 12 months free of charge.

Name Mr/Mrs/Ms ....

Address ....

....

....

.... Postcode ....

Free Print - see overleaf

Would you like to find out more about Francis Frith?

We have recently recruited some entertaining speakers who are happy to visit local groups, clubs and societies to give an illustrated talk documenting Frith's travels and photographs. If you are a member of such a group and are interested in hosting a presentation, we would love to hear from you.

Our speakers bring with them a small selection of our local town and county books, together with sample prints. They are happy to take orders. A small proportion of the order value is donated to the group who have hosted the presentation. The talks are therefore an excellent way of fundraising for small groups and societies.

Can you help us with information about any of the Frith photographs in this book?

We are gradually compiling an historical record for each of the photographs in the Frith archive. It is always fascinating to find out the names of the people shown in the pictures, as well as insights into the shops, buildings and other features depicted.

If you recognize anyone in the photographs in this book, or if you have information not already included in the author's caption, do let us know. We would love to hear from you, and will try to publish it in future books or articles.

Our production team

Frith books are produced by a small dedicated team at offices in the converted Grade II listed 18th-century barn at Teffont near Salisbury, illustrated above. Most have worked with the Frith Collection for many years. All have in common one quality: they have a passion for the Frith Collection. The team is constantly expanding, but currently includes:

Jason Buck, John Buck, Douglas Burns, Heather Crisp, Isobel Hall, Rob Hames, Hazel Heaton, Peter Horne, James Kinnear, Tina Leary, Hannah Marsh, Eliza Sackett, Terence Sackett, Sandra Sanger, Shelley Tolcher, Susanna Walker, Clive Wathen and Jenny Wathen.